For

Book design by Arlene Greco

For Tante Martha

Illustrations copyright © 1998
Diana Jackson, Licensed by Wild Apple Licensing
Text copyright © 1992, 1998
Peter Pauper Press, Inc.
202 Mamaroneck Avenue
White Plains, NY 10601
ISBN 0-88088-076-7
Printed in China
7 6 5 4 3 2 1

CONTENTS

A Little History of Felines

Here, Kitty Kitty! Here, Kitty Kitty! For thousands of years, human beings have been coaxing and cajoling—with differing degrees of success—that splendid and singular creature known as the cat.

The ancient Egyptians were the first to fall under the cat's sublime spell. They worshiped the cat in the form of the goddess *Bast*, who had the head of a cat but the body of a human; the killing of a cat was punishable by death. Pilgrims often traveled to the Temple of Bast to place mummified cats in its sanctuary, along with mummified rice and milk for the feline hereafter. When a cat died, Egyptians mourned the loss by shaving off their eyebrows. Tombs of Egyptian royalty often contained mummified cats beside the mummies of their royal masters.

Sanskrit writings reveal the cat's presence in India, and in China there is evidence that Confucius kept a cat—perhaps inspiring all his wise sayings! The cities of Carthage and Alexandria in olden times had cat populations of over 100,000.

Phoenician traders are believed to have brought the domesticated Egyptian cat to Britain around 900 B.C. The Romans considered the cat a symbol of liberty, and it followed them into Europe as the Roman Empire expanded. A European domesticated breed eventually developed from the inbreeding of the Egyptian variety with European wild cats, but it was destined to have a much more turbulent history than its Egyptian cousin.

In about 600 A.D. the Prophet Muhammad preached to the multitudes while holding a cat in his arms.

Throughout the Middle Ages, European cats, especially black ones, became associated with black magic and witches. Often cats were thought to be witches in disguise, or to be vested with the spirit of Satan that could cause harm to people while they slept. The cat thus became a dreaded creature.

It is thus not surprising that until the 17th century the French burned thousands of cats to safeguard the people from witches. King Louis XIII put a stop to it, but in the 1730s cats were ritually massacred as a social protest against the state of affairs in

Paris at the time. The French, however, were not the only perpetrators. By the 18th century, the cat was no longer a prized possession to the British either. A visitor to the Tower of London's menageries could either pay a fee or furnish a cat to be fed to the lions.

By the 1870s, though, the illustrious cat had regained its status with the Europeans. The English relied on cats to rid their country of rodents. One wealthy squire actually levied a fine (in bushels of corn) on anyone who intentionally killed a cat. In 1871, the first modern cat show was mounted at the famous Crystal Palace in London, and soon it was an annual event. It was followed by a Scottish cat show in Edinburgh in 1875. By 1895, the Americans had caught feline fever and held a full-fledged cat show at Madison Square Garden with more than 200 cats being exhibited. Today, there are over 400 cat shows staged annually throughout the United States.

It seems, at last, that after 4,000 years the cat has finally come full circle. While these days we may not rank the cat with the gods (as the Egyptians

did) it is fair to say that cat
lovers abound everywhere.

We hope you and your feline
friends enjoy our catty concoc-
tion of Dear Tabby's, cat words,
famous felines, superstitions,
cats in art and literature,
quotes, and poems.

S. B.

DEAR TABBY

Dear Tabby,

I am obsessed with a real Feline Fatale. She's gorgeous, and I would do anything to be with her. I've made a few advances, and she acts like she's interested, but then she'll ignore me for days. I'm not sure how much longer I can take these cat-and-mouse games. I'd forget her if I could, but I can't. How can I make her love me?

Signed,
At Cat Woman's Mercy

Dear At Cat Woman's Mercy,

What are you? A man or a mouse? If you continue to let your feline friend stick her claws in you, you deserve what you get. The sooner you drop her like a bad piece of fish, the better.

Dear Tabby,

I'm a mother of 16, and expecting yet another kitty litter. I love my babies, but I am tuckered out. There just doesn't seem to be time enough in the day to feed them all, clean them all, and take them all to the park. I catnap whenever I can, but it doesn't seem to help. What can I do?

> *Signed,*
> *On My Last Paw*

Dear On My Last Paw,

What you need, my dear, is a vaCATion. So drop the kits at your mother's or hire a sitter. There are lots of great places to relax and unwind. Might I suggest a few? The Catskills, Catalina Island, St. Kitts . . .

13

D E A R
T A B B Y

Dear Tabby,

I have soft black hair, glassy green eyes, and a curvaceous figure. Whenever I go out by myself, all of the toms in the neighborhood meow and make catcalls as I pass by. I don't do anything to encourage their remarks, and I wish they would stop. It isn't fair. I can't help the way I look.

Signed,
Victim of Desire

Dear Victim of Desire,

Granted, sometimes it's best just to ignore those terrible toms, but evidently that strategy hasn't worked for you. So quit pussy-footing around. The next time they start in on you, give it right back and tell them to go to Purrrgatory!

Dear Tabby,

My younger sister is driving me up a tree. Whatever I do, she copycats. If I go for a lick of milk, she goes for a lick of milk. If I wear a rhinestone collar, she wears one too. I've tried everything to get her to stop, but nothing works. Pretty soon I'm going to scratch her eyes out. HELP!

> *Signed,*
> *A Suffering Siamese*

Dear Suffering Siamese,

Younger kitties often mimic their older siblings in an attempt to seem more mature. Your sister is simply showing her admiration for you. Don't be so catty. Spend a little quality time with her—say, throwing the old ball of yarn around. She might feel less ignored, and give you your space.

15

CAT DICTIONARY

CAT·NIP	Feline love bite
CAT·WALK	Pussy prowl
CAT·TY	"Meow-Meow"
CAT·KIN	Feline Family
POPO·**CAT**·EPETL	Mexican Cat with volcanic temper
DE·**CAT**·HLON	Track and field event at Cat Olympics
HEP·**CAT**	Katharine's favorite feline
CAT·TISH	Four-fifths feline
CAT·TY-CORNER	When Tom has Jerry in a jam

CAT·CALL	Feline 'fone conversation
CAT·HODE·RAY	Permits Cable TUBETV for pussycats
CAT·ABOLISM	Feline blood pressure, digestion, etc.
CAT·ACLYSM	Two toms out at night
CAT·ALYTIC CONVERTER	Changes a kitten into a cat
CAT·ALEPSY	When a cat sleeps 22 hours a day
CAT·AMOUNT	Pussy peak overlooking Katmandu
CAT·ALOG	Cat's Diary

CAT·AMARAN	Boat for the owl and the pussycat
CAT·SUP	A relish for pet food
CAT·ATONIC	Feline summer drink
CAT·EGORY	A horror story about cats
CAT·ASTROPHY	Award for catching a mouse
CAT·SKILL	Tabby talent
CAT·TLE	They say "meow" instead of "moo."
CAT·ALYST	Feline phone book

CAT·ENATION	Kitty kingdom
KITTY HAWK	Capital of Catenation
CAT·ARACTS	Imperfect pupils
CAT·NAP	The big sleep
CAT'S·CRADLE	Love game
CAT·CHER	Four-legged baseball player
CAT·TAIL	Kitty legend
KAT·MANDU	Capital of Nepalese cats
CAT·ACOMB	Used with a CATABRUSH

FAMOUS FELINES

Morris the Cat, the talking cat of advertising fame

Garfield, of the comic strip

Cat in the Hat, courtesy of Dr. Seuss

Pink Panther, immortalized in human form by Peter Sellers

Cowardly Lion, Dorothy's furry friend

Puss in Boots, the sly, boot-wearing cat of the fairy tale

Tony the Tiger, spokescat for Frosted Flakes

Cheshire Cat, Alice's smiling companion

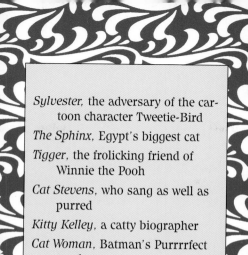

Sylvester, the adversary of the cartoon character Tweetie-Bird

The Sphinx, Egypt's biggest cat

Tigger, the frolicking friend of Winnie the Pooh

Cat Stevens, who sang as well as purred

Kitty Kelley, a catty biographer

Cat Woman, Batman's Purrrrfect crook

Tom, of the cat and mouse duo, Tom and Jerry

Felix the Cat, famed cartoon character since the 1920s

Heathcliff, the tough little cat of the comics

Sayings about Cats

A cat has nine lives.

Ancient peoples were amazed that cats always landed on their feet, even from "impossible" positions. Modern scientists, using high-speed photography, have shown that the spine of the cat is incredibly supple, and that all parts of the cat move in harmony to achieve a landing "on all fours."

When the cat's away, the mice will play.

Just ask the babysitter!

Honest as a cat when the cream is out of reach.

People are honest too, unless there is money lying on the street. The saying denotes a person who is not to be trusted.

Even a cat can look at a king.

A citizen has a vote, and the protection of the law, even if he or she is not the president or a powerful figure.

Curiosity killed the cat.

It's dangerous to be *too* curious!

The Mysterious Kitty

When the cat's away, mice may play, but when the cat's around, mysteries abound! Superstitions have always seemed to trail this reserved and independent creature.

One of the earliest and most famous superstitions is that the cat possesses nine lives. The "nine" is often believed to stem from the religious Trinity—nine being a trinity of trinities, and, therefore, particularly symbolic. The nine lives superstition has led to many unusual behaviors—such as keeping a cat aboard a boat to ward off danger.

Supernatural beliefs about cats often revolve around nighttime. People have throughout history endowed the cat with the ability to see in the dark because its eyes appear to glow at night. (Cats see no better in the dark than the average human, but their eyes do gather and reflect whatever light is available.)

Cats are also associated with the moon. Moon myths arose from a story about the Greek goddess *Artemis* (later named *Diana* by the Romans), who, being chased by a monster named *Typhon*, changed herself into a cat and hid in the moon. Here also lies the basis for the many folk tales of women, and especially witches, metamorphosing into cats.

Even cat hairs are brushed with superstition! In the Ozarks of mid-America, cat hairs can determine whether a girl should accept a proposal of marriage. The young lady simply plucks three hairs from a cat's tail, wraps them in paper, and places them at her front door. If, in the morning, the three hairs appear to form a "Y," she accepts. If they seem to form an "N," she declines.

A cat hair supposedly can also be used to cure ailments. One example is that of using a hair from the tail of a black cat to relieve a swollen eyelid or sty. The hair must be plucked on the first night of a full moon (of course!) and stroked across the ailing lid nine times (of course, again!).

THE ARTISTIC KITTY

Since the Egyptians first took a fancy to the feline, artists have been inspired by cats. An Egyptian tomb drawing from approximately 2,600 B.C. is one of the first works of art to feature a cat. Later Egyptians produced sculptures of cats in bronze and other materials. Cats are a particular favorite of the artists of France and East Asia. The French Impressionist Pierre August Renoir painted his *Girl with a Cat,* Theodore Gericault did *Studies of a Cat* in pencil, and Gustave Courbet is known for his *Woman with a Cat.* The 18th century Japanese artist Ichiryusai Hiroshige often depicted his feline model in woodblock prints.

Modern American artists from Norman Rockwell to Andrew Wyeth have focused their attention on the cat. Sculptures by Edward F. Hoffman III and Heinz Warneke, and oil paintings such as *Black Panther* by Alice Dineen and *Hot Milk: Waiting for It to Cool* by Elisabeth F. Bonsall are examples.

THE LITERARY KITTY

As the cat has made a strong showing in the art world, so also has the feline graced the pages of literature! Since cats first arrived in Aesop's fables, kitties have been appearing, or disappearing (like Lewis Carroll's Cheshire Cat!), in the literary realm. Among these famous fictional cats are Beatrix Potter's tidy, housekeeping cat Simkins, Edgar Allan Poe's Pluto, Saki's gossipy pussycat Tobermory, Charles Dickens' beastly Lady Jane from *Bleak House*, and, of course, Puss in Boots, the crafty hero of the fairy tale by Perrault.

While perhaps the most famous collection of kitty poems is T. S. Eliot's *Old Possum's Book of Practical Cats*, there are heaps of other verses featuring cats, from children's nursery rhymes to William Butler Yeats' Minnaloushe who danced by moonlight.

And there is no need to worry about the future; advertisements for the hit Broadway musical boldly proclaim: "Cats—Now and Forever."

POETRY, PROSE, AND
NURSERY RHYMES ABOUT CATS

I like little Pussy, her coat is so
    warm,
And if I don't hurt her she'll do me
    no harm;
So I'll not pull her tail, nor drive
    her away,
But Pussy and I very gently will
    play.

Source unknown

Ding, dong, bell,
Pussy's in the well;
Who put her in?
Little Tommy Green,
Who pulled her out?
Little Johnny Stout.

Nursery rhyme

As I was going to St. Ives,
I met a man with seven wives,
Each wife had seven sacks,
Each sack had seven cats,
Each cat had seven kits:
Kits, cats, sacks, and wives,
How many were there going to St.
    Ives?

Nursery rhyme

Sing, sing,
What shall I sing?
The cat's run away
With the pudding string!
Do, do,
What shall I do?
The cat's run away
With the pudding too!

Nursery rhyme

When the tea is brought at five
    o'clock,
And all the neat curtains are drawn
    with care,
The little black cat with bright
    green eyes
Is suddenly purring there.

Harold Monro,
Milk for the Cat

Dame Trot and her cat
Sat down for a chat;
The Dame sat on this side
And puss sat on that.

Puss, says the Dame,
Can you catch a rat,
Or a mouse in the dark?
Purr, says the cat.

Nursery rhyme

Pussy cat, pussy cat,
Where have you been?
I've been to London
To visit the queen.
Pussy cat, pussy cat,
What did you there?
I frightened a little mouse
Under her chair.

Nursery rhyme

There was a young lady of Riga,
Who went for a ride on a tiger;
They returned from the ride
With the lady inside,
And a smile on the face of the tiger.

Anonymous

Poor Matthias! Would'st thou have
More than pity? claim'st a stave!
—Friends more near us than a bird
We dismissed without a word,

Rover, with the good brown head,
Great Atossa, they are dead;
Dead, and neither prose nor rhyme
Tells the praises of their prime.
Thou did'st know them old and grey,
Knew them in their sad decay.
Thou hast seen Atossa sage
Sit for hours beside thy cage;
Thou would'st chirp, thou foolish bird,
Flutter, chirp—she never stirr'd!
What were now these toys to her?
Down she sank amid her fur;
Eyed thee with a soul resign'd—
And thou deemedst cats were kind!
—Cruel, but composed and bland,
Dumb, inscrutable and grand,
So Tiberius might have sat,
Had Tiberius been a cat.

Matthew Arnold,
Poor Matthias

Hey diddle diddle,
The cat and the fiddle,
The cow jumped over the moon;
The little dog laughed
To see such sport,
And the dish ran away with the
    spoon.

Mother Goose

THE OWL AND THE PUSSY-CAT

The Owl and the Pussy-Cat went to
sea
    In a beautiful pea-green boat:
They took some honey, and plenty
of money
    Wrapped up in a five-pound
    note.
The Owl looked up to the stars
above,

And sang to a small guitar
"O lovely Pussy, O Pussy, my love,
　　What a beautiful Pussy you are,
　　　　You are,
　　　　You are,
　　What a beautiful Pussy you are!"

Pussy said to the Owl, "You elegant
fowl,
　　How charmingly sweet you sing!
Oh! let us be married; too long we
have tarried:
　　But what shall we do for a
　　ring?"

They sailed away, for a year and a
day,
　　To the land where the bong-tree
　　grows;
And there in a wood a Piggy-wig
stood,

With a ring at the end of his
nose,
    His nose,
    His nose,
With a ring at the end of his
nose.

"Dear Pig, are you willing to sell for
one shilling
    Your ring?" Said the Piggy, "I
    will."
So they took it away, and were married next day
    By the Turkey who lives on the
    hill.
They dined on mince and slices of
quince,
    Which they ate with a runcible
    spoon;
And hand in hand, on the edge of
the sand,

They danced by the light of the
moon,
    The moon,
    The moon,
They danced by the light of the
moon.

Edward Lear

SONNET TO MRS. REYNOLDS' CAT

Cat, who has passed the grand
    climacteric,
How many mice and rats hast in
    thy days
Destroyed? How many titbits
    stolen?
        Gaze
With those bright languid segments
    green, and prick
Those velvet ears—but prithee do

not stick
Thy latent claws in me—and
    upraise
Thy gentle mew—and tell me all thy
    frays
Of fish and mice and rats and ten-
    der chicks.
Nay, look not down, nor lick thy
    dainty wrists.
For all the wheezy asthma, and for
    all
Thy tail's tip is nicked off, and
    though the fists
Of many a maid have given thee
    many a maul
        Still is thy fur as when
        the lists
In youth thou enterd'st on glass-
    bottled wall.

John Keats

THE MASTER'S CAT

One evening we were all, except father, going to a ball, and when we started, we left "the Master" and his cat in the drawing-room together. "The Master" was reading at a small table; suddenly the candle went out. My father, who was much interested in his book, relighted the candle, stroked the cat, who was looking at him pathetically he noticed, and continued his reading. A few minutes later, as the light became dim, he looked up just in time to see puss deliberately put out the candle with his paw, and then look appealingly at him. This second and unmistakable hint was not disregarded and puss was given the petting he craved.

Charles Dickens' daughter Mary,
My Father as I Recall Him

THE CAT THAT WALKED BY HIMSELF

Next day the Cat waited to see if any other Wild Thing would go up to the Cave, but no one moved in the Wet Wild Woods, so the Cat walked there by himself; and he saw the Woman milking the Cow, and he saw the light of the fire in the Cave, and he smelt the smell of the warm white milk.

Cat said, "O my Enemy and Wife of my Enemy, where did Wild Cow go?"

The Woman laughed and said,
"Wild Thing out of the Wild Woods,
go back to the Woods again, for I
have braided up my hair, and I
have put away the magic blade-
bone, and we have no more need of
either friends or servants in our
Cave."

Cat said, "I am not a friend, and I
am not a servant. I am the Cat who
walks by himself, and I wish to
come into your Cave."

Woman said, "Then why did you
not come with First Friend on the
first night?"

Cat grew very angry and said, "Has
Wild Dog told tales of me?"

Then the Woman laughed and said, "You are the Cat who walks by himself, and all places are alike to you. You are neither a friend nor a servant. You have said it yourself. Go away and walk by yourself in all places alike."

Then Cat pretended to be sorry and said, "Must I never come into the Cave? Must I never sit by the warm fire? Must I never drink the warm white milk? You are very wise and very beautiful. You should not be cruel even to a Cat."

Woman said, "I knew I was wise, but I did not know I was beautiful. So I will make a bargain with you. If ever I say one word in your

praise, you may come into the
Cave."

"And if you say two words in my
praise?" said the Cat.

"I never shall," said the Woman,
"but if I say two words in your
praise, you may sit by the fire in
the Cave."

"And if you say three words?" said
the Cat.

"I never shall," said the Woman,
"but if I say three words in your
praise, you may drink the warm
white milk three times a day for
always and always and always."

Then the Cat arched his back and said, "Now let the Curtain at the mouth of the Cave, and the Fire at the back of the Cave, and the Milk-pots that stand beside the Fire, remember what my Enemy and the Wife of my Enemy has said." And he went away through the Wet Wild Woods waving his wild tail and walking by his wild lone.

Rudyard Kipling

The Hen & the Cat

A sly Cat, who had caught more than one chick in her day, hearing that a Hen was laid up sick in her nest, paid her a visit of condolence. She crept up to the nest and said softly: How are you, my dear friend? what can I do for you? what are you in want of? only tell me, if there is anything in the world that I can bring you. But you must keep up your spirits, and don't be alarmed. Thank you, said the Hen; but if you will be good enough to leave me alone, and ask your sisters to do likewise, I have no doubt but I shall soon be well enough. *The good wishes of an enemy make the wise man nervous.*

Aesop

THE QUOTABLE CAT

We've got a cat called Ben Hur. We called it Ben 'til it had kittens.
Sally Poplin

Balanchine has trained his cat to perform brilliant *jetés* and *tours en l'air*; he says that at last he has a body worth choreographing for.
Bernard Taper

Every dog has its day, but the nights are reserved for the cats.
Anonymous

It's easy to understand why the cat has eclipsed the dog as modern America's favorite pet. People like pets to possess the same qualities they do. Cats are irresponsible and recognize no authority, yet are completely dependent on others for their material needs. Cats cannot be made to do anything useful. . . . In fact, cats possess so many of the same qualities as some people . . . that it's often hard to tell the people and the cats apart.

P. J. O'Rourke,
Modern Manners

Cats, like men, are flatterers.
Walter Savage Landor

When a cat is alone she never
purrs.

Samuel Johnson

Cats are intended to teach us that
not everything in nature has a
function.

Garrison Keillor

If a cat spoke, it would say things
like "Hey, I don't see the *problem*
here."

Roy Blount, Jr.

Cat: a pygmy lion who loves mice,
hates dogs, and patronizes human
beings.

Oliver Herford

A cat cares for you only as a source of food, security and a place in the sun. Her high self-sufficiency is her charm.

Charles Horton Cooley

It would be a very good thing for the cat occasionally to find itself chased by the mouse.

Anthony Berkeley

However superior to any number of cats a mouse may feel in its own hole, it requires a good deal of self-suggestion to maintain this opinion in the presence of the cat.

Anthony Berkeley

We tie bright ribbons around their necks, and occasionally little tinkling bells, and we affect to think that they are as sweet and vapid as the coy name "kitty" by which we call them would imply. It is a curious illusion. For, purring beside our fireplaces and pattering along our back fences, we have got a wild beast as uncowed and uncorrupted as any under heaven.

Alan Devoe

Cats are such good friends—they ask no questions, they accept no criticisms.

Edna Beilenson

I will admit to feeling exceedingly
proud when any cat has singled me
out for notice; for, of course, every
cat is really the most beautiful
woman in the room. That is part of
their deadly fascination.

E. V. Lucas

A baited cat may grow as fierce as a
lion.

Samuel Palmer

By associating with the cat one
only risks becoming richer.

Colette

Are cats lazy? Well, more power to them if they are. Which one of us has not entertained the dream of doing just as he likes, when and how he likes, and as much as he likes?

Fernand Mery

If a fish is the movement of water embodied, given shape, then cat is a diagram and pattern of subtle air.

Doris Lessing

DINOSAURS

Copyright © 2005 Top That! Publishing plc.

tangerine
Press

an imprint of

SCHOLASTIC
www.scholastic.com

Scholastic and Tangerine Press and associated logos are trademarks of Scholastic Inc.
Published by Tangerine Press, an imprint of Scholastic Inc., 557 Broadway, New York, NY 10012
10 9 8 7 6 5 4 3 2 1
0-439-78526-X
Printed and bound in China

24 Contents

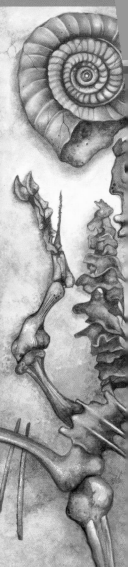

What is a Dinosaur?

Dinosaurs were a group of animals that lived on Earth until about 65 million years ago.

Scary Monsters
Many of the best-known dinosaurs were enormous, fearsome hunters with huge, sharp teeth and claws. Some were very large, while others were tiny.

Reptiles
Dinosaurs were reptiles. Like the reptiles alive today, they laid eggs and had scaly skin, but unlike their modern relatives, they had long legs underneath their bodies.

Terrible Lizards
It is only since Victorian times that we have begun to properly understand dinosaurs. In 1841, it was a British scientist, Professor Richard Owen, who discovered that dinosaurs were a group of many different animals. He named the dinosaurs—"terrible lizards," and his discovery changed the way people think about life on Earth.

Many Breeds
Many other types of (now extinct) reptiles lived at the same time as the dinosaurs.

Fascinating
Today, we are still fascinated by these incredible and often terrifying creatures.

Dinosaurs lived on Earth for about 185 million years—about 90 times longer than humans have been around. The time period in which they lived is called the Mesozoic Era.

The Mesozoic Era is divided into three periods—the Triassic, Jurassic, and Cretaceous.

Coelophysis lived in the Triassic period.

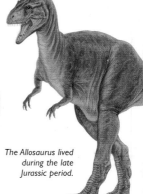

The Jurassic world, 206–144 million years ago.

Triassic Period
250–206 million years ago

This is the time when the dinosaurs first appeared—small, two-legged meat-eaters and larger plant-eaters. All the land on Earth was joined together in one huge continent that we call Pangaea. The weather was dry and warm, and leafy trees and plants flourished. Other animals included insects, crocodiles and small mammals.

Jurassic Period
206–144 million years ago

This was the time of some of the greatest-ever dinosaurs—mainly huge plant-eaters.

The Triassic world, 250–206 million years ago.

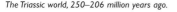

The Allosaurus lived during the late Jurassic period.

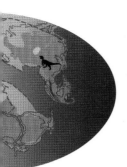

Cretaceous Period
144–65 million years ago

The land had almost split into how it is today. The weather continued to get colder, dividing into wet and dry seasons.

The first flowering plants appeared, and many large predatory (hunting) dinosaurs lived at this time. By the end of this period, the dinosaurs had died out.

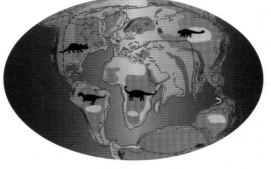

The Cretaceous world, 144–65 million years ago.

Pangaea was beginning to split into separate continents divided by oceans. The weather became cooler and, huge forests began to appear. The first birds appeared and the sky was full of huge, flying reptiles called pterosaurs.

The Tyrannosaurus rex lived during the late Cretaceous period.

After dinosaurs died, they gradually became buried under many layers of sand or mud, which eventually became rock. Dinosaur bones and teeth were preserved in the rock as fossils. By looking at fossils, we learn more about dinosaurs and other prehistoric creatures.

Delicate Diggers

Scientists who study dinosaur fossils are called palaeontologists. Sometimes they work in teams to search an area where they think they will find fossils. Many fossils are discovered by accident, and these are sent to a palaeontologist to be studied. Detailed records are made of the site, and the fossil is handled very carefully.

Fossils have been found on every continent on Earth.

A palaeontologist identifying a fossil.

"Dem Bones"

Dinosaur bones can tell us a lot. It's easy to get an idea of what a dinosaur looked like and how big it was from a complete skeleton. Claws and armor will show how it attacked, and defended itself, and the skull will provide clues to what it ate.

Dinner Time!

Dinosaur teeth can tell us about their diet.

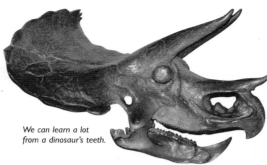

We can learn a lot from a dinosaur's teeth.

Meat-eaters generally had long, sharp teeth for tearing flesh; plant-eaters' teeth tended to be wider and flatter.

Scaly Skin

Although the skin of dinosaurs has not survived, some fossils have been found with the patterns and texture of the skin imprinted on the rock.

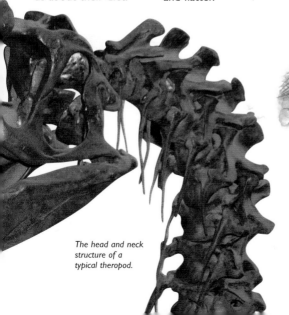

The head and neck structure of a typical theropod.

Changing Color

We can only guess the color of dinosaurs, which may have depended on the need for camouflage. Some may have been able to change color to warn off others or to attract a mate.

It is difficult to discover much about dinosaur behavior and lifestyle from their remains, but many fossil sites contain the remains of large numbers of dinosaurs.

A scavenging Tyrannosaurus rex.

Plant-Eating Herds

The fact that plant-eaters were found together suggests that they lived in herds or packs. Plant-eaters probably lived in herds for safety reasons.

Pack Hunters

A large pack of carnivores (meat-eaters) would be able to hunt more effectively than individuals.

Lone Hunters

Tyrannosaurus rex was probably a lone hunter, ambushing its prey with its mouth wide open.

A pack of Coelophysis hunting prey.

Egg Layers

Most dinosaurs, like reptiles today, laid eggs. Large numbers of fossilized eggs have been found together, meaning that some dinosaurs may have nested together in large groups, or colonies. There is some evidence to suggest that, like birds, they may have returned to the same place to nest year after year.

A nest of baby dinosaurs.

Big Brood

Dinosaurs would have had many babies, but it is thought that very few of them would have been caring parents. One possible exception is the group of dinosaurs known as hadrosaurs. There is evidence to suggest that their young looked very cute—they had big eyes and rounded heads—so their parents may have been more likely to look after them.

A baby hadrosaur.

A hadrosaur tending to her young.

Dinosaurs were one of the most successful groups of animals that ever lived on Earth. Then, about 65 million years ago, something happened that wiped them out.

Volcanic eruptions may have killed off the dinosaurs.

Theories
There are many theories about what exactly happened, but most experts agree that it was very sudden and that it affected the whole planet—its climate, plants, and animals other than the dinosaurs.

Meteorite
A popular theory is that the Earth was hit by a huge meteorite or asteroid from outer space.

The meteorite's impact would have caused an explosion, sending up enormous clouds of dust into the atmosphere. This would have blocked the sun, creating a long, worldwide winter. Without light and heat, millions of plants and animals would have died, including the dinosaurs.

Large clouds of dust could have blocked out light and heat.

Volcanic Eruptions
Other experts suggest that volcanic eruptions may be responsible. These could have burned up the oxygen in the atmosphere, making it difficult for living things to breathe.

Deadly Disease
Some experts think that dinosaur extinction was a slower process. Some kind of deadly disease could have killed them, or changing vegetation may have poisoned them to death. Also, the new types of mammals that were appearing may have eaten the dinosaur eggs.

Putting dinosaurs into different groups is not easy. There are many different types and the relationships between them are not always clear. Plus, new research about dinosaurs often changes their names or places them in different groups.

Ornithischians had pubis bones that pointed downward and to the front, like those of birds.

An Ornithiscian pubis bone.

Division

Dinosaurs are normally divided into two main orders (groups) which classify them according to the shape of their hip bones. The groups are called Saurischia ("lizard-hipped") and Ornithischia ("bird-hipped").

In a Saurischian skeleton, the pubis bone of the hip points down and to the back, like that of a lizard.

A Saurischian pubis bone.

Meat and Plant

Saurischians are divided into two groups: the fast, meat-eating theropods and the large, plant-eating sauropods. The sauropods appeared first but the theropods remained until the end of the dinosaur age.

Tyrannosaurus rex was a theropod—a Saurischian dinosaur.

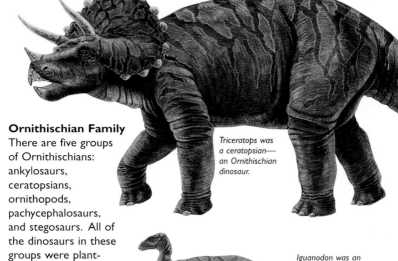

Ornithischian Family

There are five groups of Ornithischians: ankylosaurs, ceratopsians, ornithopods, pachycephalosaurs, and stegosaurs. All of the dinosaurs in these groups were plant-eaters and some developed armor plating, horns or spikes to defend themselves against predators.

Triceratops was a ceratopsian—an Ornithischian dinosaur.

Iguanodon was an ornithopod—an Ornithischian dinosaur.

The Bird Question

Interestingly, birds are believed to have evolved from the Saurischians, rather than the Ornithischians (see page 35).

Euoplocephalus was an ankylosaur—an Ornithischian dinosaur.

13

The theropod group of Saurischian dinosaurs contained some of the most fearsome carnivorous (meat-eating) creatures ever to walk the Earth, including *Allosaurus* (pages 30–31) and *Tyrannosaurus rex* (pages 32–33).

Large Hunters

These large hunters all walked (and ran) on their rear legs—the front legs were often tiny. Their heads were large, and their mouths were filled with many razor-sharp teeth. Their long tails helped them to balance.

Fearsome Find

One of the first theropods to be identified and named was *Megalosaurus*, which means "big reptile." Remains were found in Oxfordshire, England, in 1824.

Hunters and Scavengers

While the largest of the theropods probably hunted and scavenged for food alone, some of the smaller ones are thought to have hunted in packs. *Deinonychus* was one such creature. Its name means "terrible claw," which describes the lethal curved claws that it had on the second toe of each foot. A group of *Deinonychus* would leap on their prey and slash at it.

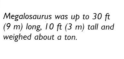
Megalosaurus was up to 30 ft (9 m) long, 10 ft (3 m) tall and weighed about a ton.

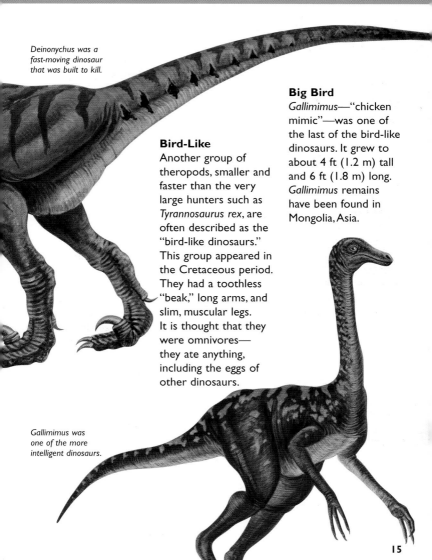

Deinonychus was a fast-moving dinosaur that was built to kill.

Big Bird

Gallimimus—"chicken mimic"—was one of the last of the bird-like dinosaurs. It grew to about 4 ft (1.2 m) tall and 6 ft (1.8 m) long. *Gallimimus* remains have been found in Mongolia, Asia.

Bird-Like

Another group of theropods, smaller and faster than the very large hunters such as *Tyrannosaurus rex*, are often described as the "bird-like dinosaurs." This group appeared in the Cretaceous period. They had a toothless "beak," long arms, and slim, muscular legs. It is thought that they were omnivores— they ate anything, including the eggs of other dinosaurs.

Gallimimus was one of the more intelligent dinosaurs.

15

The sauropods included some of the largest creatures ever to walk the Earth. Appearing during the Jurassic period, these enormous vegetarians had long necks and tails and bulky bodies. They walked on all four legs, but could rear up on to their back legs to reach the leaves of tall trees. As the sauropods evolved, they got bigger and bigger. The biggest of all was *Brachiosaurus* (pages 40–41).

Brachiosaurus was the tallest of the sauropods.

Stretch and Reach
Diplodocus is one of the best-known of this type of dinosaur. It was quite slim for a sauropod, but was one of the longest, measuring up to 89 ft (27 m) mainly due to its long neck and tail.

Down in One

Sauropods' teeth were a bit like clothes pegs—long and flat and not use for chewing. They closed their mouth around the leaves of trees, and stripped them off, swallowing them whole.

Astrodon (meaning "star-tooth") was a long-necked, plant-eating sauropod that is known only from fossilized teeth found in the state of Maryland.

Diplodocus' long neck was probably used to get to food that other sauropods couldn't reach.

Quick-Footed

No one is really sure why the sauropods grew to be so large, but such huge creatures were less likely to suffer attacks from smaller predators. Despite their size, it is thought that sauropods could move quite quickly. Their foot bones were similar to those of modern elephants—large animals able to move at high speed. However, it is unlikely that they were able to run.

Balancing Act

A sauropod's skeleton was immensely strong. The weight of the long neck and tail was balanced over the back legs.

Ankylosaurs

The Ornithischian ankylosaurs were small to medium-sized dinosaurs. The main feature of these plant-eaters, which lived during the Cretaceous period, was their armor of bony plates or spikes.

These would have been especially useful when the dinosaur was being attacked by a large, vicious predator.

Armored Tanks
Ankylosaurs had broad, low bodies and were covered in bony, patterned plates. Their heads were small and heavily armored. It is thought that ankylosaurs had a good sense of smell.

Several of the ankylosaurs, including *Polacanthus* and *Ankylosaurus* (see pages 44–45), had spikes.

Safety First
It is thought that *Polacanthus* would crouch low to the ground, using its spiked armor to protect itself.

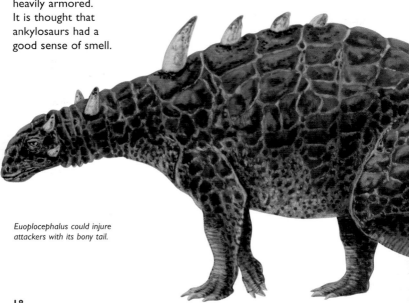

Euoplocephalus could injure attackers with its bony tail.

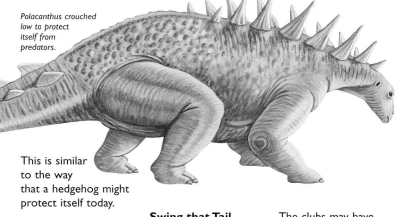

Polacanthus crouched low to protect itself from predators.

This is similar to the way that a hedgehog might protect itself today.

A hedgehog's spikes work like an ankylosaur's spikes.

Swing that Tail

Some ankylosaurs, including the *Euoplocephalus* and *Ankylosaurus*, had a bony club at the end of their tails. A powerful swing of the tail could easily topple, or even injure, a large theropod attacker.

The clubs may have measured up to 3 ft (1 m) across. The muscles of an ankylosaur's tail would have been extremely powerful.

Sink or Swim

It is thought that ankylosaurs tended to avoid areas where there were lots of rivers and lakes, as their heavy armor would have made swimming almost impossible.

Ceratopsians

The ceratopsians were a group of plant-eaters that appeared during the Cretaceous period. They had a sharp, beak-like mouth, much like a parrot. Their teeth were good for chewing, as were their powerful jaws.

Triceratops.

Efficient Eating
The ceratopsians were able to eat the toughest of plants, such as the flowering magnolia plants that began to appear in the Cretaceous period.

Globe Trotters
Many remains of *Protoceratops* have been found in Mongolia. These range from complete

nests of eggs, to the bones of adults.

Effective Armor
The most distinctive features of most of the ceratopsians were the horns on their heads and the bony plate above their necks. These would have been useful for

defending themselves from an attack by predators, but many dinosaur experts think that they were mainly used for fighting each other. It's easy to imagine a pair of rival male *Centrosaurus'* or *Triceratops'* (see pages 46–47) locked in battle like deer today.

Centrosaurus had a large single nose horn, like a rhinoceros.

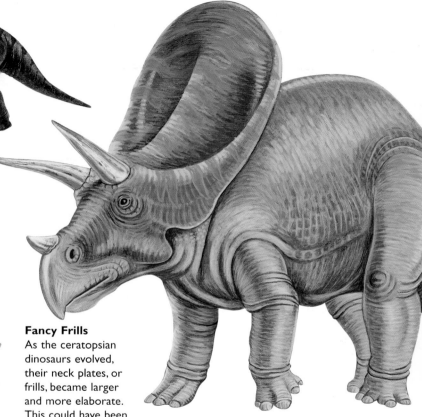

Fancy Frills
As the ceratopsian dinosaurs evolved, their neck plates, or frills, became larger and more elaborate. This could have been for "social" reasons. Ceratopsians were most likely to be herd animals and a large, fancy-looking frill might have shown who was the leader of a group.

Showing Off
Torosaurus had the largest frill of any of the ceratopsians—longer even than its own skull, which in itself was up to 8½ft (2.6 m) long!

Torosaurus had a reduced nose horn and well-developed eyebrow horns.

21

The group of dinosaurs known as the ornithopods includes one of the first dinosaurs to be studied, *Iguanodon* (see pages 38–39), and a further family of dinosaurs called hadrosaurs.

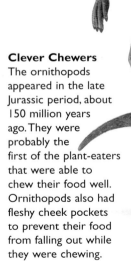

Hadrosaurs were the only dinosaurs whose teeth were continually replaced by new ones.

Clever Chewers

The ornithopods appeared in the late Jurassic period, about 150 million years ago. They were probably the first of the plant-eaters that were able to chew their food well. Ornithopods also had fleshy cheek pockets to prevent their food from falling out while they were chewing.

Puffed Up

The hadrosaurs are known for their duck-like beaks and various strangely shaped skulls. *Edmontosaurus* had loose flaps of skin that they could inflate, probably to communicate and show off.

Getting Attention

Parasaurolophus was the hadrosaur with the most extremely developed head.

The long, curved crest on the top of its skull was hollow and connected to its nose. These were much larger in males, and it is thought that they were used to create a long, hooting sound. The bigger the crest, the louder the hoot!

Safety in Numbers

None of the ornithopods appear to have had many ways of defending themselves, but they do seem to have lived together in large groups, which may have given some protection and suggests they were social creatures.

Swift Swimmers

The hadrosaurs had quite wide, paddle-shaped hands, which could have been used for swimming. This trait would have provided a useful method of escape.

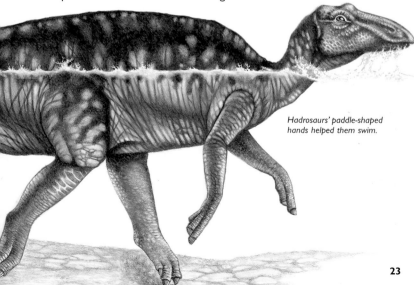

Hadrosaurs' paddle-shaped hands helped them swim.

23

Known as the "head-banging" dinosaurs, the pachycephalosaurs appeared toward the end of the dinosaur age, in the late Cretaceous period. Their skulls had a thick dome on the top, which was up to 10 in (25 cm) thick.

The skull of a pachycephalosaur.

Little Guys
The majority of the group were relatively small—*Stegoceras* being only 8 ft (2.4 m) long. However, *Pachycephalosaurus* was an impressive 15 ft (4.6 m) in length.

Shock Tactics
The extremely thick skulls of the pachycephalosaurs were probably used to ram attackers, or as many experts believe, in displays of strength.

Head-butting competitions would take place, in order to impress the females in their group.

Good Support

The very heavy skull was connected to the rest of the body in a way that would have supported it well and absorbed the shock of head-butting. Its neck bones were very thick.

Scant Remains

Skeletons and other remains of pachycephalosaurs are rarely found—an entire skeleton is yet to be discovered. Most of the remains have been found in North America. Most experts think that the lack of fossilized remains means that they probably lived in very dry areas—places where remains would not be very well preserved.

Boneheads

The skull of a pachycephalosaur makes it look like a large-brained, intelligent creature. Unfortunately, with so much of it being made of bone, these dinosaurs are known as the "boneheads."

A pair of pachycephalosaurs fighting.

The stegosaurs are named after the best-known member of the group—*Stegosaurus* (pages 42–43). They are identified by the rows of bony plates along the length of their back.

It was once thought that the plates lay flat on the stegosaur's back like the tiles on a roof—"stegosaur" means "roof lizard."

Holey Plates
It is unlikely that the plates would have protected stegosaurs from an attack, as they are not solid but have honeycomb-like cavities (spaces) inside.

Solar Panels
Scientists believe that they would have been used to help the stegosaur control its body temperature. They would have helped it funnel a breeze over its body to cool down, and to collect heat from the sun when it was too cold.

Easy Target
Stegosaurs were large, slow-moving creatures that fed on vegetation, mostly on the ground. It is thought that they would have been an easy target for predators. Their only

form of defense was their heavily-spiked tails, which they would swing using its powerful muscles.

The skeleton of a stegosaur.

Asian Discovery

Several complete stegosaur skeletons have been found in China. *Tuojiangosaurus* is one of the best-known examples and was the first stegosaur ever to be discovered in Asia. It had all the classic features of a stegosaur. Most of the weight of the animal was supported on its rear legs.

Stegosaurus weighed about 6,800 lbs (3,100 kg).

27

***Coelophysis* is one of the earliest-known dinosaurs, living around 220 million years ago. It was small, lightly-built and walked on its rear legs. It was probably very fast. Its hollow bones and long legs made it very light and quite athletic.**

Not Fussy
As a carnivore, its speed would have been very useful. Like many meat-eaters, *Coelophysis* was probably a scavenger as well. Fossilized remains of small reptiles and fish have been found inside

The Coelophysis would have been approximately two-thirds as tall as a man.

them. There is also some evidence that they would they would have eaten each other!

Snake-Like Neck
Coelophysis had a very long, narrow head and jaws at the end of a long neck. It had lots of very sharp, serrated (saw-like) teeth. Its arms had useful, grasping hands with fingers strong enough to grasp prey.

Desert Living
In 1947, Edwin Colbert's discovery of the first complete *Coelophysis* skeleton was followed by the discovery of many more remains at Ghost Ranch, New Mexico. This turned out to be a massive bone bed, containing several complete skeletons.

Coelophysis

Group:	Saurischia, theropod
Height:	4 ft (1.2 m)
Length:	10 ft (3 m)
When it lived:	Triassic period, 210 million years ago
Fossils found in:	North America

Space Dinosaur
A *Coelophysis* skull from the Carnegie Museum of Natural History was taken into space by the space shuttle *Endeavour* in 1998. It spent time on the space station *Mir*.

Coelophysis means "hollow form." This dinosaur had light, hollow bones.

The complete fossilized remains of a Coelophysis.

29

Allosaurus was a large, powerful meat-eater with a massive tail. Its vertebrae (back bones) were different from other similar dinosaurs, a fact that gives *Allosaurus* its name— "different reptile."

Allosaurus had large, powerful jaws with long, sharp teeth up to 2–4 in (5–10 cm) long.

"Top Dog"

Its arms were short, but were quite strong with long claws. Like other large theropods, it had big, powerful jaws with very sharp teeth. Its skull was about 3 ft (90 cm) long and it had bony brows and ridges above its eyes. It probably hunted and ate small to medium-sized sauropods and was the top predator in the Jurassic period. They were not rivalled in size until the tyrannosaurs appeared in the Cretaceous period.

Lie in Wait

The big question about *Allosaurus* and other large meat-eaters is whether they could have run very fast. Many scientists believe that if the *Allosaurus* fell over at speed, it would injure itself very badly. It is therefore more likely that *Allosaurus* would hide and wait for its prey to get near and then pounce. Slower, injured animals would have been its most likely targets.

What's for Dinner?

Whichever way *Allosaurus* caught its food, seeing it eat would have been a terrifying sight. Its powerful jaw and neck muscles allowed it to tear huge lumps of flesh from its victims and swallow them whole. After a big meal, *Allosaurus* would have laid down on the ground and basked in the sun.

Group:	Saurischia, theropod
Height:	16 ½ ft (5 m)
Length:	39 ft (11.9 m)
When it lived:	Late Jurassic period, 150 million years ago
Fossils found in:	North America, Australia

Tyrannosaurus Rex

Tyrannosaurus rex—"the lizard king" is probably the best-known of all the dinosaurs, as it is always featured in movies and stories about prehistoric creatures, such as *The Land That Time Forgot* and *Jurassic Park*.

It is famous as the biggest predator ever to have lived on land, although others have since been discovered (*Giganotosaurus*, pages 36–37) that are bigger.

Replacement Teeth
Despite losing its crown as the biggest meat-eater, *T. rex* was still one of the fiercest predators. Its huge mouth was filled with very strong, pointed teeth that were up to 23 cm (9 in.) long. Its teeth were replaced as they wore down or broke off.

Greedy Guts
They were capable of crunching bone and scientists think that they were able to swallow as much as 500 lbs (230 kg) of meat and bone at once!

T. rex had a stride length up to 15 ft (4.6 m).

The enormous skull was about 5 ft (1.5 m) long.

32

Tyrannosaurus Rex

Heavy Mover

As with the other large theropods, there is some mystery about the speed a *T. rex* could run. Some scientists think that it could have run at up to 15 mph (24 kph). *T. rex's* tail may have helped to control it at speed, as it was slim and stiff and helped the dinosaur balance.

Tiny Arms

For such a fearsome beast, the *T. rex* had tiny little arms and claws, which were not much use. It is thought that *T. rex* may therefore have had a problem getting up if it fell over.

Group:	Saurischia, theropod
Height:	20 ft (6 m)
Length:	46 ft (14 m)
When it lived:	Late Cretaceous period, 70 million years ago
Fossils found in:	North America

Compsognathus was the smallest of all known dinosaurs, weighing only 8 lbs (3–6 kg). Most of the skeletons found are about the size of a large chicken, though both larger and smaller examples exist.

Dino Digits
Its arms were short and it had two clawed fingers on each hand. Each foot included a tiny toe pointing backward.

Run For It
Compsognathus was one of the bird-like theropods and, being so small and with hollow bones, it would have been a very fast runner. It ate meat, chewing up insects and small lizards with its tiny, sharp teeth. It would have been a good scavenger—easily able to find scraps and able to escape larger predators and outrun other scavengers.

Forest Forage
Compsognathus probably lived in dense, forested areas where there was plenty of food and where it could hide from larger creatures.

Bird Mystery

Compsognathus is an important part of one of the great dinosaur mysteries— did birds evolve from them? The skeleton of *Compsognathus* is very similar to that of a feathered, bird-like creature, *Archaeopteryx*.

Archaeopteryx lived at about the same time as *Compsognathus* and had feathered wings with claws at the end. Scientists are still trying to work out if it was a bird (it probably could not fly) or simply a dinosaur with wings.

Bird or dinosaur?

Compsognathus was a bird-like dinosaur designed for speed.

Group:	Saurischia, theropod
Height:	Up to 2 ft (60 cm)
Length:	Up to 4 ½ ft (1.3 m)
When it lived:	Late Jurassic period, 150 million years ago
Fossils found in:	Germany, France

Giganotosaurus was the biggest meat-eater ever to walk the Earth. It lived about 30 million years before its close relative, Tyrannosaurus rex.

Fearsome Hunter
The teeth of *Gigantosaurus* were about 8 in (20 cm) long. They were sharp and knife-like.

Banana Brain
Weighing in at about eight tons, *Giganotosaurus* was literally gigantic. Although it was bigger than *T. rex*, it was more lightly built and could have been able to move more quickly. It also had a much smaller brain than *T. rex*, about the size and shape of a banana.

Gigantosaurus weighed about 8 tons.

Group:	Saurischia, theropod
Height:	Up to 25 ft (7.6 m)
Length:	Up to 50 ft (15 m)
When it lived:	Cretaceous period, 100 million years ago
Fossils found in:	South America

What a Find

A complete *Giganotosaurus* has not yet been found. The first discovery of its remains was in Argentina in 1994. Its name means "giant southern lizard." It was discovered not by an expert palaeontologist, but by a car mechanic whose hobby was looking for dinosaur fossils. His name was Ruben Carolini, and this huge dinosaur has been given the scientific name *Giganotosaurus carolinii* in his honor.

The fossils of the *Iguanodon* were among the first to be discovered. They were found in England in 1809—before the word "dinosaur" had been invented. Their discoverer, Gideon Mantell, realized that the teeth were similar to those of the iguana—a modern lizard.

Large Brain

For a dinosaur, it had quite a large brain and good senses. It is thought that they may have lived in social groups and cared well for their young.

Human Habits

Iguanodon was a fairly large, plant-eating dinosaur. At the front of its mouth was a horned, toothless beak which it used to nip at vegetation. At the back, in its cheeks, were many rows of teeth. These were excellent for chewing a wide range of plants. It is thought that *Iguanodon* chewed and swallowed its food in much the same way as people do.

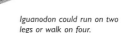

Iguanodon could run on two legs or walk on four.

Iguanodon's teeth were at the back of the mouth.

Group:	Saurischia, theropod
Height:	16 ft (4.8 m)
Length:	30 ft (9.1 m)
When it lived:	Early Cretaceous period, 130 million years ago
Fossils found in:	Britain, North Africa, Asia

Fingers and Thumbs

Iguanodon's arms were long and strong. They had hands with four fingers and a thumb. They would have walked either on two legs or on all fours. The thumb was equipped with a large spike, which was used for defense and finding food. It might also have been used to fight rivals in the same social group.

Brachiosaurus was the tallest and largest of all the massive, plant-eating sauropods. Walking on all four legs, it used its very long neck and long front legs to reach the leaves at the tops of trees, and had a posture very similar to the giraffe.

Heavyweights

These huge creatures were among the heaviest of all dinosaurs, weighing up to 88 tons. The legs of the *Brachiosaurus* had to bear all the weight of the body while moving. We refer to such creatures as "graviportal" or "heavy carrying."

Water Wonder

It used to be thought that *Brachiosaurus* spent most of its time in water, much like hippos today.

Its nostrils were placed high on its forehead, suggesting that they could have been used a bit like a snorkel. While most scientists now agree that it lived on land, there is some evidence that it would have waded in lakes and rivers. It may have done this to feed on

water plants. It is thought that healthy adult *Brachiosaurus* were safe from predators. They were twice the size of the

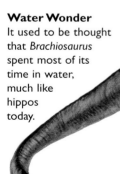

meat-eating theropods that lived at the time, and there was plenty of easier prey around.

The legs of the Brachiosaurus had to bear all the weight while moving.

Stone Swallowers

A great many *Brachiosaurus* (and other sauropods) skeletons have been found with small stones in their stomachs. It is thought that these were swallowed by the young dinosaur to help it mash up and digest food in its stomach.

Group:	Saurischia, sauropod
Height:	39 ft (11.8 m)
Length:	74 ft (22.5 m)
When it lived:	Jurassic period, 150 million years ago
Fossils found in:	North America, Africa

The largest of all the stegosaurs, *Stegosaurus* is famous for the plates on its back and also for its small brain—the smallest of all the dinosaurs.

Mate Plate

Stegosaurus had 17 bony plates on its back and tail. As well as controlling body temperature (see pages 26–27), it's possible that the males used their plates to attract a mate.

Angry Tail

Stegosaurs' spiked tails were used as weapons. The tail had eight of these spikes, each up to 4 ft (1.2 m) long.

Attention

Some scientists believe the plates would blush during courting. This would also happen when a fight was imminent as a threat display. Scientists are unsure whether the plates laid flat or upright.

Stegosaurus' back legs were twice as long as its front legs.

Group:	Ornithischia, stegosaur
Height:	Up to 15 ½ ft (4.7 m)
Length:	Up to 30 ft (9.1 m)
When it lived:	Jurassic period, 150 million years ago
Fossils found in:	North America

Walnut Brain

Stegosaurus is famous for having a very small brain—often described as being the "size of a walnut." Scientists compare the size of a dinosaur's brain with the rest of its body to guess its intelligence. As *Stegosaurus* was very large (as big as a large truck), it was probably not very clever.

Predators

This herbivore would have been preyed on by the fierce carnivore *Allosaurus* (pages 30–31).

Weighing around 4.4 tons, *Ankylosaurus* was the largest member of the ankylosaur family, the "fused together lizards." It lived at the end of the age of the dinosaurs.

It lived at the same time as the fearsome *Tyrannosaurus rex* (see pages 32–33), a dinosaur that was probably one of its predators.

Heavy Duty
Ankylosaurus was heavily protected by its bony plates and spikes. Even its eyes were protected.

Soft Underbelly
The only way a predator would have been able to attack *Ankylosaurus* would be to flip it over— its underbelly was unprotected. Most would probably give up and look for easier prey.

The Pink One
As with the plates of a *Stegosaurus*, the body armor of this dinosaur may also have turned pink after being filled with blood, earning it the nickname the "blushing dinosaur."

Ankylosaurus had low intelligence compared to other dinosaurs.

Ankylosaurus

Pardon Me!

Ankylosaurus' diet was limited to the plants that it found close to the ground. Some scientists think that this meant its stomach would have produced an enormous amount of gas!

Group:	Ornithischia, ankylosaur
Height:	10 ft (3 m)
Length:	33 ft (10 m)
When it lived:	Late Cretaceous period, 70 million years ago
Fossils found in:	North and South America

Triceratops—"three-horned face"—is one of the best-known dinosaurs. Living at the end of the dinosaur age, it was the largest of the ceratopsians. It is often compared to the rhinoceros of today. An adult *Triceratops* however, would be around twice the size of a rhino.

Fighting

It is thought that the horns were used to fight rivals, but they would have been an excellent way of attacking a predator. It would have charged at its attacker (*T. rex* lived at the same time), in much the same way as a rhino does.

Bony

The bony horns and neck plate are the most distinctive features of *Triceratops* and most of the other ceratopsians. It had one short horn above its parrot-like beak and two longer horns, just above its eyes.

Triceratops had a large skull, up to 10 ft (3 m) long.

Group:	Ornithischia, ceratopsian
Height:	13 ft (4 m)
Length:	30 ft (9.1 m)
When it lived:	Late Cretaceous period, 70 million years ago
Fossils found in:	North America

Bit Common

Triceratops was a very common dinosaur and many fossil examples have been found, mostly in western North America. When the fossils were first discovered in the late 19th century, they were thought to belong to an extinct species of buffalo.

Research into dinosaurs is going on all the time. Fossils are found, palaeontologists discuss theories about them and new ways of studying dinosaurs are developed.

Museums

Museums all over the world have displays of some of the best dinosaur remains. Many of them have complete skeletons and life-size models of dinosaurs. This is the best way to see what these incredible creatures were like for yourself.

On Screen

Dinosaurs continue to be the subject of science fiction films. Some of them have suggested that dinosaur remains could be used to bring them back to life. Scientists all agree that this is impossible... for now!